DAMN!
A Book of Calumny
BY H · L · MENCKEN

PHILIP GOODMAN · NEW YORK · 1918

Fourth Edition

PREFACE

The title borne by this little book was not my invention, and got my *imprimatur* only rather grudgingly and at the last moment. I consented to it, in fact, simply to avoid a long and costly telegraphic debate with the publisher, from whom I was separated by 200 miles. The "Damn" part seemed to me to be too heavily devilish and *sforzando*—a fit label for a book by a sensational gentleman of God or a wicked college professor. As for the "Book of Calumny" part, it plainly misrepresented the work itself, which is chiefly devoted, not to calumniating things, but to defending and praising them. Thus, I even go so far as to speak for alcohol, war and the Jews, all of which are usually execrated. Still more, I argue that 99 per cent. of the married men of America are faithful to their wives: a doctrine absolutely novel, and so much at odds with current superstition as to appear almost ironical.

So the title, from the start, has libelled the book, which is moral and reassuring in character, and not only libelled it, but also brought down upon it the indignation of the right-thinking. For example, the New York *Times,* after printing one advertisement of it, refused to print any more—on the sound ground that a book so named, and of contents fitting the title, would surely outrage the pruderies of its subscribers. Again, a great many newspaper critics, too hard worked to read so small a book, wrote their reviews upon its cover, and so fell into lamentable misrepresentations. Thus the critic of the Salt Lake *Republican* called it "devilishly slanderous," where its actual tone, as I have said, is one of encomium and inspiration. Thus the critic of the Philadelphia *Public Ledger* described it as full of "foolish things" said in "moments of exasperation," whereas there is not the slightest sign of exasperation in it, but only a

mellow forbearance. Thus the Spring-
field *Republican* denounced it as "cynical and immoral," and the St. Louis
Post-Dispatch as "written by a pessimist
solely for pessimists," and the Chicago
Daily News as "strutting and squalling,"
whereas it is obviously not cynical or immoral or pessimistic, but full of high hope
and rectitude, and not strutting and
squalling, but extremely polite and *pia-
nissimo*. Finally, various estimable view-
ers with alarm, mistaking its theology for
politics, complained of it as seditious,
whereas the plain fact is that its very first
chapter is given over to a defense of
George Washington.

In order to dispose of such misunder-
standings I have been tempted to change
the title, but to this the publisher objects.
Part of his objection is perfectly logical:
the change would put him to expense and
expose him to the charge of trying to sell
the same book twice. But part of it, I
fancy, is also due to considerations a good
deal less benign. A book violently en-

titled has plain advantages, on the book-counters, over books more decorous; it arrests the eye and gives wings to the dollar. Perhaps some such notion floats in my own mind, too, and so accounts for my own complaisance; I am also a hypocrite. But after all it is a small matter. The substance of the work is moral enough, and it can stand an inappropriate title. Who really cares what the title is? Who really cares, indeed, what the book is? In all the range of nature there is no phenomenon intrinsically more trivial. Not one book in a thousand is worth as much to mankind as an innocent little child or a Chicago ham. Not all the books written in a century have impinged upon human history as potently as the invention of the bichloride tablet.

Several reviewers have speculated as to my reasons for printing a volume so odd in size and make up—a few score casual essays, some longish, some telegraphically brief, scarcely two hanging together. My explanation is very simple. It was thus that the thing came into my mind, and I saw no good reason for laboring it into some other form. I said what I had to say upon each topic that presented itself, and then shut down. If any other ideas ever occur to me I shall simply write another book.

MENCKEN.

Baltimore, July, 1918.

CONTENTS

DAMN! · A BOOK OF · CALUMNY

I.

PATER PATRIÆ

If George Washington were alive today, what a shining mark he would be for the whole camorra of uplifters, forward-lookers and other such inspired Bolsheviki! He was the Rockefeller of his time, the richest man in the United States, a promoter of companies, a land-magnate, an exploiter of mines and timber. He had a liking for all forthright and pugnacious men, and a contempt for lawyers, reformers and other such obscurantists. He was not pious. He drank whisky whenever he felt chilly, and kept a jug of it handy. He knew far more profanity than Scripture, and used and enjoyed it more. He had no belief in the infallible wisdom of the lower classes, but regarded them as inflammatory dolts, and tried to save the republic from them. He advo-

13

cated no sure cure for all the sorrows of the world, and doubted that such a panacea existed. He took no interest in the private morals of his neighbors.

Inhabiting These States today, George would be ineligible to any office of honor or profit. The Senate would never dare confirm him; the President could not think of nominating him. He would be on trial in all the yellow journals for belonging to the Invisible Government, the Hell Hounds of Plutocracy, the Money Power, the Interests. The Sherman Act would have him in its toils; he would be under indictment by every grand jury south of the Potomac; the triumphant prohibitionists of his native state would be denouncing him (he had a still at Mount Vernon) as a debaucher of youth, a recruiting officer for insane asylums, a poisoner of the home. The suffragettes would be on his trail, with sentinels posted all along the Accotink road. The initiators and referendors would be bawling for his blood. The young college men of the

Nation and the *New Republic* would be lecturing him weekly. He would be used to scare children in Kansas and Arkansas. The chautauquas would shiver whenever his name was mentioned. . . .

And what a chance there would be for that ambitious young district attorney who thought to shadow the greatest man the New World has ever produced—and grab him under the Mann Act!

II

THE REWARD OF THE ARTIST

A man labors and fumes for a whole
year to write a symphony in G minor. He
puts enormous diligence into it, and much
talent, and maybe no little downright
genius. It draws his blood and wrings his
soul. He dies in it that he may live again.
. . . Nevertheless, its final value, in the
open market of the world, is a great deal
less than that of a fur overcoat, half a
Rolls-Royce automobile, or a handful of
authentic hair from the whiskers of
Henry Wadsworth Longfellow.

III

THE HEROIC CONSIDERED

For humility and poverty, in themselves, the world has little liking and less
respect. In the folk-lore of all races, despite the sentimentalization of abasement
for dramatic effect, it is always power and
grandeur that count in the end. The
whole point of the story of Cinderella, the
most widely and constantly charming of
all stories, is that the Fairy Prince lifts
Cinderella above her cruel sisters and
stepmother, and so enables her to lord it
over them. The same idea underlies practically all other folk-stories: the essence of
each of them is to be found in the ultimate
triumph and exaltation of its protagonist.
And of the real men and women of history, the most venerated and envied are
those whose early humiliations were but
preludes to terminal glories; for example,
Lincoln, Whittington, Franklin, Jackson,
Columbus, Demosthenes, Frederick the
Great, Catherine, Mary of Magdala,

Moses. Even the Man of Sorrows, cradled in a manger and done to death between two thieves, is seen, as we part from Him at last, in a situation of stupendous magnificence, with infinite power in His hands. Even the Beatitudes, in the midst of their eloquent counselling of renunciation, give it unimaginable splendor as its reward. The meek shall inherit—what? The whole earth! And the poor in spirit? They shall sit upon the right hand of God!
. . .

IV

The Burden of Humor

What is the origin of the prejudice
against humor? Why is it so dangerous,
if you would keep the public confidence,
to make the public laugh? Is it because
humor and sound sense are essentially antagonistic? Has humanity found by experience that the man who sees the fun of
life is unfitted to deal sanely with its prob-
lems? I think not. No man had more of
the comic spirit in him than William
Shakespeare, and yet his serious reflec-
tions, by the sheer force of their sublime
obviousness, have pushed their way into
the race's arsenal of immortal platitudes.
So, too, with Æsop, and with Balzac, and
with Dickens, to come down the scale.
All of these men were fundamentally
humorists, and yet all of them achieved
what the race has come to accept as a
penetrating sagacity. Contrariwise, many
a haloed pundit has had his occasional
guffaw. Lincoln, had there been no Civil

19

War, might have survived in history chiefly as the father of the American smutty story—the only original art-form that America has yet contributed to literature. Huxley, had he not been the greatest intellectual duellist of his age, might have been its greatest satirist. Bismarck, pursuing the gruesome trade of politics, concealed the devastating wit of Moliere; his surviving epigrams are truly stupendous, and a Frenchman, Jules Hoche, has written a whole book on his larger buffooneries. Finally, Beethoven, after soaring to the heights of tragedy in the first movement of the Fifth Symphony, turned to the sardonic bull-fiddling of the *scherzo*.

No, there is not the slightest disharmony between sense and nonsense, humor and respectability, despite the skittish tendency to assume that there is. But, why, then, that widespread error? What actual fact of life lies behind it, giving it a specious appearance of reasonableness? None other, I am convinced, than the fact that the average man is far too stupid to make a joke. He may *see* a joke and *love* a joke, particularly when it floors and flabbergasts some person he dislikes, but the only way he can himself take part in the priming and pointing of a new one is by acting as its target. In brief, his personal contact with humor tends to fill him with an accumulated sense of disadvantage, of pricked complacency, of sudden and crushing defeat; and so, by an easy psychological process, he is led into the idea that the thing itself is incompatible with true dignity of character and intellect. Hence his deep suspicion of jokers, however adept their thrusts. "What a damned fool!"—this same half-pitying tribute he pays to wit and butt alike. He cannot separate the virtuoso of comedy from his general concept of comedy itself, and that concept is inextricably mingled with memories of foul ambuscades and mortifying hurts. And so it is not often that he is willing to admit any wisdom in a humorist, or to condone frivolity in a sage.

V

The Saving Grace

Let us not burn the universities—yet. After all, the damage they do might be worse. . . . Suppose Oxford had snared and disemboweled Shakespeare! Suppose Harvard had rammed its buttermilk into Mark Twain!

VI

Moral Indignation

The loud, preposterous moral crusades that so endlessly rock the republic—against the rum demon, against Sunday baseball, against moving-pictures, against dancing, against fornication, against the cigarette, against all things sinful and charming—these astounding Methodist jehads offer fat clinical material to the student of mobocracy. In the long run, nearly all of them must succeed, for the mob is eternally virtuous, and the only thing necessary to get it in favor of some new and super-oppressive law is to convince it that that law will be distasteful to the minority which it envies and hates. The poor numskull who is so horribly harrowed by Puritan pulpit-thumpers that he can't go to a ball game on Sunday afternoon without dreaming of hell and the devil all Sunday night is naturally envious of the fellow who can, and being envious of him, he hates him and is eager

23

to destroy his offensive happiness. The farmer who works 18 hours a day and never gets a day off is envious of his farm-hand who goes to the crossroads and barrels up on Saturday afternoon; hence the virulence of prohibition among the peasantry. The hard-working householder who, on some bitter evening, glances over the *Saturday Evening Post* for a square and honest look at his wife is envious of those gaudy drummers who go gallivanting about the country with scarlet girls; hence the Mann Act. If these deviltries were equally open to all men, and all men were equally capable of practising and appreciating them, their unpopularity would tend to wither.

I often think, indeed, that the prohibitionist tub-thumpers make a tactical mistake in dwelling too much upon the evils and horrors of alcohol, and not enough upon its delights. A few enlarged photographs of first-class bar-rooms, showing the rows of well-fed, well-dressed *bibuli* happily moored to the brass rails, their noses in fragrant mint and hops and their hands reaching out for free rations of olives, pretzels, cloves, pumpernickle, Bismarck herring, anchovies, wieners, Smithfield ham and dill pickles—such a gallery of contentment would probably do far more execution among the dismal *shudra* than all the current portraits of drunkards' livers. To vote for prohibition in the face of the liver portraits means to vote for the good of the other fellow, for even the oldest bibulomaniac always thinks that he himself will escape. This is an act of altruism almost impossible to the mobman, whose selfishness is but little corrupted by the imagination that shows itself in his betters. His most austere renunciations represent no more than a matching of the joys of indulgence against the pains of hell; religion, to him, is little more than synthesized fear . . . . I venture that many a vote for prohibition comes from gentlemen who look longingly through swinging doors—and pass on in propitia-

tion of Satan and their alert consorts, the
lake of brimstone and the corrective
broomstick. . . .

VII.

STABLE-NAMES

Why doesn't some patient drudge of a *Privat Dozent* compile a dictionary of the stable-names of the great? All show dogs and race horses, as everyone knows, have stable-names. On the list of entries a fast mare may appear as Czarina Olga Fedorovna, but in the stable she is not that at all, nor even Czarina or Olga, but maybe Lil or Jennie. And a prize bulldog, Champion Zoroaster or Charlemagne XI. on the bench may be plain Jack or Ponto *en famille*. So with celebrities of the *genus homo*. Huxley's official style and appellation was "The Right Hon. Thomas Henry Huxley, P. C., M. D., Ph. D., LL. D., D. C. L., D. Sc., F. R. S.," and his biographer tells us that he delighted in its rolling grandeur—but to his wife he was always Hal. Shakespeare, to his fellows of his Bankside, was Will, and perhaps Willie to Ann Hathaway. The Kaiser is another Willie: the late Czar

27

so addressed him in their famous exchange of telegrams. The Czar himself was Nicky in those days, and no doubt remains Nicky to his cronies today. Edgar Allan Poe was always Eddie to his wife, and Mark Twain was always Youth to his. P. T. Barnum's stable-name was Taylor, his middle name; Charles Lamb's was Guy; Nietzsche's was Fritz; Whistler's was Jimmie; the late King Edward's was Bertie; Grover Cleveland's was Steve; J. Pierpont Morgan's was Jack; Dr. Wilson's is Tom.

Some given names are surrounded by a whole flotilla of stable-names. Henry, for example, is softened variously into Harry, Hen, Hank, Hal, Henny, Enery, O'nry and Heine. Which did Ann Boleyn use when she cooed into the suspicious ear of Henry VIII.? To which did Henrik Ibsen answer at the domestic hearth? It is difficult to imagine his wife calling him Henrik: the name is harsh, clumsy, razor-edged. But did she make it Hen or Rik, or neither? What was

Bismarck to the Fürstin, and to the mother he so vastly feared? Ottchen? Somehow it seems impossible. What was Grant to his wife? Surely not Ulysses! And Wolfgang Amadeus Mozart? And Rutherford B. Hayes? Was Robert Browning ever Bob? Was John Wesley ever Jack? Was Emanuel Swendeborg ever Manny? Was Tadeusz Kosciusko ever Teddy?

A fair field of inquiry invites. Let some laborious assistant professor explore and chart it. There will be more sweet fancy in his report than in all the novels ever written.

VIII

THE JEWS

The Jews, like the Americans, labor
under a philosophical dualism, and in
both cases it is a theological heritage. On
the one hand there is the idealism that is
lovely and uplifting and will get a man
into heaven, and on the other hand there
is the realism that works. The fact that
the Jews cling to both, thus running, as it
were, upon two tracks, is what makes
them so puzzling, now and then, to the
goyim. In one aspect they stand
for the most savage practicality; in
another aspect they are dreamers of
an almost fabulous other-worldliness.
My own belief is that the essential Jew is
the idealist—this his occasional flashing of
hyena teeth is no more than a necessary
concession to the harsh demands of the
struggle for existence. Perhaps, in many
cases, it is due to an actual corruption of
blood. The Jews come from the Levant,
and their women were exposed for many

centuries to the admiration of Greek, Arab and Armenian. The shark that a Jew can be at his worst is simply a Greek or Armenian at his best.

As a statement of post-mortem and super-terrestial fact, the religion that the Jews have foisted upon the world seems to me to be as vast a curse as the influenza that we inherit from the Tartars or the political fallacies set afloat by the French Revolution. The one thing that can be said in favor of it is that it is not true, and yet we suffer from it almost as much as if it were true. But with it, encasing it and preserving it, there has come something that is positively valuable — something, indeed, that is beyond all price—and that is Jewish poetry. To compare it to the poetry of any other race is wholly impossible; it stands completely above all the rest; it is as far beyond the next best as German music is beyond French music, or French painting beyond English painting, or the English drama beyond the Italian drama. There are single chapters in the

Old Testament that are worth all the poetry ever written in the New World and nine-tenths of that written in the Old. The Jews of those ancient days had imagination, they had dignity, they had ears for sweet sound, they had, above all, the faculty of grandeur. The stupendous music that issued from them has swept their barbaric demonology along with it, setting at naught the collective intelligence of the human species; they embalmed their idiotic taboos and fetishes in undying strains, and so gave them some measure of the same immortality. A race of lawgivers? Bosh! Leviticus is as archaic as the Code of Manu, and the Decalogue belongs to ethical paleontology. A race of seers? Bosh again! The God they saw survives only as a bogeyman, a theory, a gaseous vertebrate, an uneasy and vexatious ghost. A race of traders and sharpers? Bosh a third time! The Jews are as poor as the Spaniards. But a race of poets, my lords, a race of poets! It is a vision of beauty that has ever haunted them. And it has been their destiny to transmit that vision, enfeebled, perhaps, but still distinct, to other and lesser peoples, that life might be made softer for the sons of men, and the goodness of the Lord God—whoever He may be—might not be forgotten.

IX

The Comstockian Premiss

It is argued against certain books, by virtuosi of moral alarm, that they depict vice as attractive. This recalls the king who hanged a judge for deciding that an archbishop was a mammal.

X

THE LABIAL INFAMY

After five years of search I have been able to discover but one book in English upon the art of kissing, and that is a very feeble treatise by a savant of York, Pa., Dr. R. McCormick Sturgeon. There may be others, but I have been quite unable to find them. Kissing, for all one hears of it, has not attracted the scientists and literati; one compares its meagre literature with the endless books upon the other phenomena of love, especially divorce and obstetrics. Even Dr. Sturgeon, pioneering bravely, is unable to get beyond a sentimental and trivial view of the thing he vivisects, and so his book is no more than a compendium of mush. His very description of the act of kissing is made up of sonorous gabble about heaving bosoms, red lips, electric sparks and such-like imaginings. What reason have we for believing, as he says, that the lungs are "strongly expanded" during the act? My own casual observation inclines me to hold that the opposite is true, that the lungs are actually collapsed in a pseudo-asthmatic spasm. Again, what is the ground for arguing that the lips are "full, ripe and red?" The real effect of the emotions that accompany kissing is to empty the superficial capillaries and so produce a leaden pallor. As for such salient symptoms as the temperature, the pulse and the rate of respiration, the learned pundit passes them over without a word. Mrs. Elsie Clews Parsons would be a good one to write a sober and accurate treatise upon kissing. Her books upon "The Family" and "Fear and Conventionality" indicate her possession of the right sort of learning. Even better would be a work by Havelock Ellis, say, in three or four volumes. Ellis has devoted his whole life to illuminating the mysteries of sex, and his collection of materials is unsurpassed in the world. Surely there must be an enormous mass of instructive stuff about kissing in his card indexes, letter files, book presses and archives.

Just why the kiss as we know it should have attained to its present popularity in Christendom is probably one of the things past finding out. The Japanese, a very affectionate and sentimental people, do not practise kissing in any form; they regard the act, in fact, with an aversion matching our own aversion to the family tooth-brush. Nor is it in vogue among the Moslems, nor among the Chinese, who countenance it only as between mother and child. Even in parts of Christendom it is girt about by rigid taboos, so that its practise tends to be restricted to a few occasions. Two Frenchmen or Italians, when they meet, kiss each other on both cheeks. One used to see, indeed, many pictures of General Joffre thus bussing the heroes of Verdun; there even appeared in print a story to the effect that one of them objected to the scratching of his moustache. But imagine two Englishmen kissing! Or two Germans!

As well imagine the former kissing the latter! Such a display of affection is simply impossible to men of Northern blood; they would die with shame if caught at it. The Englishman, like the American, never kisses if he can help it. He even regards it as bad form to kiss his own wife. The Latin has no such compunctions. He leaps to the business regardless of place or time; his sole concern is with the lady. Once, in driving from Nice to Monte Carlo along the lower Corniche road, I passed a hundred or so open taxi-cabs containing man and woman, and fully 75 per cent. of the men had their arms around their companions, and were kissing them. These were not peasants, remember, but well-to-do persons. In England such a scene would have caused a great scandal; in most American States the police would have charged the offenders with drawn revolvers.

The charm of kissing is one of the things I have always wondered at. I do not pretend, of course, that I have never

done it; mere politeness forces one to it;
there are women who sulk and grow bel-
licose unless one at least makes the motions
of kissing them. But what I mean is
that I have never found the act a tenth
part as agreeable as poets, the authors of
musical comedy librettos, and (on the
contrary side) chaperones and the *gendar-
merie* make it out. The physical sensation, far from being pleasant, is intensely
uncomfortable—the suspension of respiration, indeed, quickly resolves itself into a
feeling of suffocation—and the posture
necessitated by the approximation of lips
and lips is unfailingly a constrained and
ungraceful one. Theoretically, a man
kisses a woman perpendicularly, with
their eyes, those "windows of the soul,"
synchronizing exactly. But actually, on
account of the incompressibility of the
nasal cartilages, he has to incline either
his or her head to an angle of at least 60
degrees, and the result is that his right
eye gazes insanely at the space between her
eyebrows, while his left eye is fixed upon

some vague spot behind her. An instantaneous photograph of such a maneuvre, taken at the moment of incidence, would probably turn the stomach of even the most romantic man, and force him, in sheer self-respect, to renounce kissing as he has renounced leap-frog and walking on stilts.

But the most embarrassing moment, in kissing, does not come during the actual kiss (for at that time the sensation of suffocation drives out all purely psychical feelings), but immediately afterward. What is one to say to the woman then? The occasion obviously demands some sort of remark. One has just received (in theory) a great boon; the silence begins to make itself felt; there stands the fair one, obviously waiting. Is one to thank her? Certainly that would be too transparent a piece of hypocrisy, too flaccid a banality. Is one to tell her that one loves her? Obviously, there is danger in such assurances, and beside, one usually doesn't, and a lie is a lie. Or is one to descend to chatty

commonplaces—about the weather, literature, politics, the war? The practical im-
possibility of solving the problem leads
almost inevitably to a blunder far worse
than any merely verbal one: one kisses
her again, and then again, and so on, and
so on. The ultimate result is satiety, re-
pugnance, disgust; even the girl gets
enough.

XI

A True Ascetic

"Herbert Spencer's objection to swearing, of which so much has been made by moralists, was not an objection to its sinfulness but an objection to its charm. In brief, he feared comfort, satisfaction, joy. The boarding houses in which he dragged out his gray years were as bare and cheerless as so many piano boxes. He avoided all the little vices and dissipations which make human existence bearable: good eating, good drinking, dancing, tobacco, poker, poetry, the theatre, personal adornment, philandering. He was insanely suspicious of everything that threatened to interfere with his work. Even when that work halted him by the sheer agony of its monotony, and it became necessary for him to find recreation, he sought out some recreation that was as unattractive as possible, in the hope that it would quickly drive him back to work again. Having to choose between methods of locomotion on his holidays, he chose going afoot, the most laborious and least satisfying available. Brought to bay by his human need for a woman, he directed his fancy toward George Eliot, probably the most unappetizing woman of his race and time. Drawn irresistibly to music, he avoided the Fifth Symphony and "Tristan und Isolde," and joined a crowd of old maids singing part songs around a cottage piano. John Tyndall saw clearly the effect of all this and protested against it, saying, "He'd be a much nicer fellow if he had a good swear now and then"—*i. e.,* if he let go now and then, if he yielded to his healthy human instincts now and then, if he went on some sort of debauch now and then. But what Tyndall overlooked was the fact that the meagreness of his recreations was the very element that attracted Spencer to them. Obsessed by the fear—and it turned out to be well-grounded—that he would not live long enough to complete his work, he regarded all joy as a temptation, a corruption, a sin of scarlet. He was a true ascetic.

43

He could sacrifice all things of the present for one thing of the future, all things real for one thing ideal.

XII

ON LYING

Lying stands on a different plane from all other moral offenses, not because it is intrinsically more heinous or less heinous, but simply because it is the only one that may be accurately measured. Forgetting unwitting error, which has nothing to do with morals, a statement is either true or not true. This is a simple distinction and relatively easy to establish. But when one comes to other derelictions the thing grows more complicated. The line between stealing and not stealing is beautifully vague; whether or not one has crossed it is not determined by the objective act, but by such delicate things as motive and purpose. So again, with assault, sex offenses, and even murder; there may be surrounding circumstances which greatly condition the moral quality of the actual act. But lying is specific, exact, scientific. Its capacity for precise determination, indeed, makes its presence

45

or non-presence the only accurate gauge of other immoral acts. Murder, for example, is nowhere regarded as immoral, save it involve some repudiation of a social compact, of a tacit promise to refrain from it—in brief, some deceit, some perfidy, some lie. One may kill freely when the pact is formally broken, as in war. One may kill equally freely when it is broken by the victim, as in an assault by a highwayman. But one may not kill so long as it is not broken, and one may not break it to clear the way. Some form of lie is at the bottom of all other recognized crimes, from seduction to embezzlement. Curiously enough, this master immorality of them all is not prohibited by the Ten Commandments, nor is it penalized, in its pure form, by the code of any civilized nation. Only savages have laws against lying *per se*.

XIII

HISTORY

It is the misfortune of humanity that its history is chiefly written by third-rate men. The first-rate man seldom has any impulse to record and philosophise; his impulse in to act; life, to him, is an adventure, not a syllogism or an autopsy. Thus the writing of history is left to professors, moralists, theorists, dunderheads. Few historians, great or small, have shown any capacity for the affairs they presume to describe and interpret. Gibbon was an inglorious failure as a member of Parliament. Thycydides made such a mess of his military (or, rather, naval) command that he was exiled from Athens for twenty years and finally assassinated. Flavius Josephus, serving as governor of Galilee, lost the whole province to the Romans, and had to flee for his life. Momseen, elected to the Prussian Landtag, flirted with the Socialists. How much better we would understand the habits and nature of

47

man if there were more historians like
Julius Cæsar, or even like Niccolo
Machiavelli! Remembering the sharp
and devastating character of their rough
notes, think what marvelous histories Bismarck, Washington and Frederick the
Great might have written! Such men are
privy to the facts; the usual historians
have to depend on deductions, rumors,
guesses. Again, such men know how to
tell the truth, however unpleasant; they
are wholly free of that puerile moral ob-
session which marks the pedagogue. . . .
But they so seldom tell it! Well, perhaps
some of them have—and their penalty is
that they are damned and forgotten.

XIV

THE CURSE OF CIVILIZATION

A civilized man's worst curse is social obligation. The most unpleasant act imaginable is to go to a dinner party. One could get far better food, taking one day with another, at Childs', or even in a Pennsylvania Railroad dining-car; one could find far more amusing society in a barroom or a bordello, or even at the Y. M. C. A. No hostess in Christendom ever arranged a dinner party of any pretensions without including at least one intensely disagreeable person—a vain and vapid girl, a hideous woman, a follower of baseball, a social pusher, a stockbroker, a veteran of some war or other, a gabbler of politics. And one is enough to do the business.

XV

EUGENICS

The·error of the eugenists lies in the assumption that a physically healthy man is the best fitted to survive. This is true of rats and the *pediculae,* but not of the higher animals, *e. g.,* horses, dogs and men. In these higher animals one looks for more subtle qualities, chiefly of the spirit. Imagine estimating philosophers by their chest expansions, their blood pressures, their Wasserman reactions!

The so-called social diseases, over which eugenists raise such a pother, are surely not the worst curses that mankind has to bear. Some of the greatest men in history have had them; whole nations have had them and survived. The truth about them is that, save in relatively rare cases, they do very little damage. The horror in which they are held is chiefly a moral horror, and its roots lie in the assumption that they cannot be contracted without sin. Nothing could be more false. Many great moralists have suffered from them: the gods are always up to sardonic waggeries.

Moreover, only one of them is actually inheritable, and that one is transmitted relatively seldom. But among psychic characters one finds that practically all are inheritable. For example, stupidity, credulity, avarice, pecksniffery, lack of imagination, hatred of beauty, meanness, poltroonery, petty brutality, smallness of soul. . . . I here present, of course, the Puritan complex; there flashes up the image of the "good man," that libel on God and the devil. Consider him well. If you had to choose a sire for a first-rate son, would you choose a consumptive Jew with the fires of eternity in his eyes, or an Iowa right-thinker with his hold full of Bibles and breakfast food?

XVI

The Jocose Gods

What humor could be wilder than that of life itself? Franz Schubert, on his deathbed, read the complete works of J. Fenimore Cooper. John Millington Synge wrote "Riders to the Sea" on a second-hand $40 typewriter, and wore a celluloid collar. Richard Wagner made a living, during four lean years, arranging Italian opera arias for the cornet. William Shakespeare was a social pusher and bought him a bogus coat-of-arms. Johannes Brahms had a high, piping voice and wore pantaloons that stopped at his fetlocks. Martin Luther suffered from the jim-jams. One of the greatest soldiers in Hungarian history was named Hunjadi Janos. . . .

XVII

WAR

Superficially, war seems inordinately
cruel and wasteful, and yet it must be
plain on reflection that the natural evolu-
tionary process is quite as cruel and even
more wasteful. Man's chief efforts in
times of peace are devoted to making that
process less violent and sanguinary. Civilization, indeed, may be defined as a con-
structive criticism of nature, and Huxley even called it a conspiracy against nature. Man tries to remedy what must
inevitably seem the mistakes and to check
what must inevitably seem the wanton
cruelty of the Creator. In war he aban-
dons these efforts, and so becomes more
jovian. The Greeks never represented the
inhabitants of Olympus as succoring and
protecting one another, but always as
fighting and attempting to destroy one
another.

No form of death inflicted by war is
one-half so cruel as certain forms of death

that are seen in hospitals every day. Besides, these forms of death have the further disadvantage of being inglorious. The average man, dying in bed, not only has to stand the pains and terrors of death; he must also, if he can bring himself to think of it at all, stand the notion that he is ridiculous. . . . The soldier is at least not laughed at. Even his enemies treat his agonies with respect.

XVIII

MORALIST AND ARTIST

I dredge up the following from an essay
on George Bernard Shaw by Robert
Blatchford, the English Socialist: "Shaw
is something much better than a wit, much
better than an artist, much better than a
politician or a dramatist; he is a moralist, a teacher of ethics, austere, relentless,
fiercely earnest."

What could be more idiotic?   Then
Cotton Mather was a greater man than
Johann Sebastian Bach.   Then the average college critic of the arts, with his
balderdash about inspiration and moral
purpose, is greater than George Brandes
or Saint-Beuve.   Then Eugene Brieux,
with his Y. M. C. A. platitudinizing, is
greater than Moliere, with his ethical
agnosticism, his ironical determinism.

This childish respect for moralizing
runs through the whole of contemporary
criticism—at least in England and America.   Blatchford differs from the profes-

sorial critics only in the detail that he can actually write. What he says about Shaw has been said, in heavy and suffocating words, by almost all of them. And yet nothing could be less true. The moralist, at his best, can never be anything save a sort of journalist. Moral values change too often to have any serious validity or interest; what is a virtue today is a sin tomorrow. But the man who creates a thing of beauty creates something that lasts.

XIX

ACTORS

"In France they call an actor a *m'as-tu-vu,* which, anglicised, means a have-you seen me? . . . The average actor holds the mirror up to nature and sees in it only the reflection of himself." I take the words from a late book on the so-called art of the mime by the editor of a magazine devoted to the stage. The learned author evades plumbing the psychological springs of this astounding and almost invariable vanity, this endless bumptiousness of the *cabotin* in all climes and all ages. His one attempt is banal: "a foolish public makes much of him." With all due respect, Nonsense! The larval actor is full of hot and rancid gases long before a foolish public has had a fair chance to make anything of him at all, and he continues to emit them long after it has tried him, condemned him and bidden him be damned. There is, indeed, little choice in the virulence of their self-respect between a Broadway star who is slobbered over by press agents and fat women, and the poor ham who plays thinking parts in a No. 7 road company. The two are alike charged to the limit; one more ohm, or molecule, and they would burst. Actors begin where militia colonels, Fifth avenue rectors and Chautauqua orators leave off. The most modest of them (barring, perhaps, a few unearthly traitors to the craft) matches the conceit of the solitary pretty girl on a slow ship. In their lofty eminence of pomposity they are challenged only by Anglican bishops and grand opera tenors. ╱ I have spoken of the danger they run of bursting. In the case of tenors it must sometimes actually happen; even the least of them swells visibly as he sings, and permanently as he grows older. . . .

But why are actors, in general, such blatant and obnoxious asses, such arrant posturers and wind-bags? Why is it as surprising to find an unassuming and likable fellow among them as to find a Greek without fleas? The answer is quite simple. To reach it one needs but consider the type of young man who normally gets stage-struck. Is he, taking averages, the intelligent, alert, ingenious, ambitious young fellow? Is he the young fellow with ideas in him, and a yearning for hard and difficult work? Is he the diligent reader, the hard student, the eager inquirer? No. He is, in the overwhelming main, the neighborhood fop and beau, the human clothes-horse, the nimble squire of dames. The youths of more active mind, emerging from adolescence, turn to business and the professions; the men that they admire and seek to follow are men of genuine distinction, men who have actually done difficult and valuable things, men who have fought good (if often dishonest) fights and are respected and envied by other men. The stage-struck youth is of a softer and more shallow sort. He seeks, not a chance to test his mettle by hard and useful work, but an easy chance to shine. He craves the regard, not of men, but of women. He is, in brief, a hollow and incompetent creature, a strutter and poseur, a popinjay, a pretty one. . . .

I thus beg the question, but explain the actor. He is this silly youngster grown older, but otherwise unchanged. An initiate of a profession requiring little more information, culture or capacity for ratiocination than that of the lady of joy, and surrounded in his workshop by men who are as stupid, as vain and as empty as he himself will be in the years to come, he suffers an arrest of development, and the little intelligence that may happen to be in him gets no chance to show itself. The result, in its usual manifestation, is the average bad actor—a man with the cerebrum of a floor-walker and the vanity of a fashionable chiropodist. The result, in its highest and holiest form is the actor-manager, with his retinue of press-agents, parasites and worshipping wenches—perhaps the most preposterous and awe-inspiring donkey that civilization has yet produced. To look for sense in a fellow of such equipment and such a history would be like looking for serviettes in a sailors' boarding-house.

By the same token, the relatively greater intelligence of actresses is explained. They are, at their worst, quite as bad as the generality of actors. There are she-stars who are all temperament and balderdash—intellectually speaking, beggars on horseback, servant girls well washed. But no one who knows anything about the stage need be told that it can show a great many more quick-minded and self-respecting women than intelligent men. And why? Simply because its women are recruited, in the main, from a class much above that which furnishes its men. It is after all, not unnatural for a woman of considerable intelligence to aspire to the stage. It offers her, indeed, one of the most tempting careers that is open to her. She cannot hope to succeed in business, and in the other professions she is an unwelcome and much-scoffed-at intruder, but on the boards she can meet men on an equal footing. It is therefore, no wonder that women of a relatively superior class often take to the business. . . . Once they embrace it, their superiority to their male colleagues is quickly manifest. All movements against puerility and imbecility in the drama have originated, not with actors, but with actresses—that is, in so far as they have originated among stage folks at all. The Ibsen pioneers were such women as Helena Modjeska, Agnes Sorma and Janet Achurch; the men all hung back. Ibsen, it would appear, was aware of this superior alertness and took shrewd advantage of it. At all events, his most tempting acting parts are feminine ones.

The girls of the stage demonstrate this tendency against great difficulties. They have to carry a heavy handicap in the enormous number of women who seek the footlights merely to advertise their real profession, but despite all this, anyone who has the slightest acquaintance with stagefolk will testify that, taking one with another, the women have vastly more brains than the men and are appreciably less vain and idiotic. Relatively few actresses of any rank marry actors. They find close communion with the strutting brethren psychologically impossible. Stock-brokers, dramatists and even theatrical managers are greatly to be preferred.

XX

THE CROWD

Gustave Le Bon and his school, in their discussions of the psychology of crowds, have put forward the doctrine that the individual man, cheek by jowl with the multitude, drops down an intellectual peg or two, and so tends to show the mental and emotional reactions of his inferiors. It is thus that they explain the well-known violence and imbecility of crowds. The crowd, as a crowd, performs acts that many of its members, as individuals, would never be guilty of. Its average intelligence is very low; it is inflammatory, vicious, idiotic, almost simian. Crowds, properly worked up by skilful demagogues, are ready to believe anything, and to do anything.

Le Bon, I daresay, is partly right, but also partly wrong. His theory is probably too flattering to the average numskull. He accounts for the extravagance of crowds on the assumption that the numskull, along with the superior man, is knocked out of his wits by suggestion— that he, too, does things in association that he would never think of doing singly. The fact may be accepted, but the reasoning raises a doubt. The numskull runs amuck in a crowd, not because he has been inoculated with new rascality by the mysterious crowd influence, but because his habitual rascality now has its only chance to function safely. In other words, the numskull is vicious, but a poltroon. He refrains from all attempts at lynching *a cappella,* not because it takes suggestion to make him desire to lynch, but because it takes the protection of a crowd to make him brave enough to try it.

What happens when a crowd cuts loose is not quite what Le Bon and his followers describe. The few superior men in it are not straightway reduced to the level of the underlying stoneheads. On the contrary, they usually keep their heads, and often make efforts to combat the crowd action. But the stoneheads are too many for them; the fence is torn down or the blackamoor is lynched. And why? Not because the stoneheads, normally virtuous, are suddenly criminally insane. Nay, but because they are suddenly conscious of the power lying in their numbers— because they suddenly realize that their natural viciousness and insanity may be safely permitted to function.

In other words, the particular swinishness of a crowd is permanently resident in the majority of its members—in all those members, that is, who are naturally ignorant and vicious—perhaps 95 per cent. All studies of mob psychology are defective in that they underestimate this viciousness. They are poisoned by the prevailing delusion that the lower orders of men are angels. This is nonsense. The lower orders of men are incurable rascals, either individually or collectively. Decency, self-restraint, the sense of justice, courage—these virtues belong only to a small minority of men. This minority never runs amuck. Its most distinguish-

ing character, in truth, is its resistance to
all running amuck. The third-rate man,
though he may wear the false whiskers of
a first-rate man, may always be detected
by his inability to keep his head in the face
of an appeal to his emotions. A whoop
strips off his disguise.

XXI

An American Philosopher

As for William Jennings Bryan, of whom so much piffle, pro and con, has been written, the whole of his political philosophy may be reduced to two propositions, neither of which is true. The first is the proposition that the common people are wise and honest, and the second is the proposition that all persons who refuse to believe it are scoundrels. Take away the two, and all that would remain of Jennings would be a somewhat greasy bald-headed man with his mouth open.

XXII

CLUBS

Men's clubs have but one intelligible purpose: to afford asylum to fellows who haven't any girls. Hence their general gloom, their air of lost causes, their prevailing acrimony. No man would ever enter a club if he had an agreeable woman to talk to. This is particularly true of married men. Those of them that one finds in clubs answer to a general description: they have wives too unattractive to entertain them, and yet too watchful to allow them to seek entertainment elsewhere. The bachelors, in the main, belong to two classes: (a) those who have been unfortunate in amour, and are still too sore to show any new enterprise, and (b) those so lacking in charm that no woman will pay any attention to them. Is it any wonder that the men one thus encounters in clubs are stupid and miserable creatures, and that they find their pleasure in such banal sports as playing cards, drinking highballs, shooting pool, and reading the barber-shop weeklies? ... The day a man's mistress is married one always finds him at his club.

XXIII

Fidelis ad Urnum

Despite the common belief of women to the contrary, fully 95 per cent. of all married men, at least in America, are faithful to their wives. This, however, is not due to virtue, but chiefly to lack of courage. It takes more initiative and daring to start up an extra-legal affair than most men are capable of. They look and they make plans, but that is as far as they get. Another salient cause of connubial rectitude is lack of means. A mistress costs a great deal more than a wife; in the open market of the world she can get more. It is only the rare man who can conceal enough of his income from his wife to pay for a morganatic affair. And most of the men clever enough to do this are too clever to be intrigued.

I have said that 95 per cent. of married men are faithful. I believe the real proportion is nearer 99 per cent. What women mistake for infidelity is usually no more than vanity. Every man likes to be regarded as a devil of a fellow, and particularly by his wife. On the one hand, it diverts her attention from his more genuine shortcomings, and on the other hand it increases her respect for him. Moreover, it gives her a chance to win the sympathy of other women, and so satisfies that craving for martyrdom which is perhaps woman's strongest characteristic. A woman who never has any chance to suspect her husband feels cheated and humiliated. She is in the position of those patriots who are induced to enlist for a war by pictures of cavalry charges, and then find themselves told off to wash the general's underwear.

XXIV

A Theological Mystery

The moral order of the world runs aground on hay fever. Of what use is it? Why was it invented? Cancer and hydrophobia, at least, may be defended on the ground that they kill. Killing may have some benign purpose, some esoteric significance, some cosmic use. But hay fever never kills; it merely tortures. No man ever died of it. Is the torture, then, an end in itself? Does it break the pride of strutting, snorting man, and turn his heart to the things of the spirit? Nonsense! A man with hay fever is a natural criminal. He curses the gods, and defies them to kill him. He even curses the devil. Is its use, then, to prepare him for happiness to come—for the vast ease and comfort of convalescence? Nonsense again! The one thing he is sure of, the one thing he never forgets for a moment, is that it will come back again next year.

XXV

The Test of Truth

The final test of truth is ridicule. Very few religious dogmas have ever faced it and survived. Huxley laughed the devils out of the Gadarene swine. Dowie's whiskers broke the back of Dowieism. Not the laws of the United States but the mother-in-law joke brought the Mormons to compromise and surrender. Not the horror of it but the absurdity of it killed the doctrine of infant damnation. . . . But the razor edge of ridicule is turned by the tough hide of truth. How loudly the barber-surgeons laughed at Harvey—and how vainly! What clown ever brought down the house like Galileo? Or Columbus? Or Jenner? Or Lincoln? Or Darwin? . . . They are laughing at Nietzsche yet. . . .

74

XXVI

LITERARY INDECENCIES

The low, graceless humor of names!
On my shelf of poetry, arranged by the
alphabet, Coleridge and J. Gordon Coog-
lar are next-door neighbors! Mrs.
Hemans is beside Laurence Hope! Walt
Whitman rubs elbows with Ella Wheeler
Wilcox; Robert Browning with Richard
Burton; Rosetti with Cale Young Rice;
Shelley with Clinton Scollard; Words-
worth with George E. Woodberry; John
Keats with Herbert Kaufman!

Ibsen, on the shelf of dramatists, is be-
tween Victor Hugo and Jerome K. Jer-
ome. Sudermann follows Harriet
Beecher Stowe. Maeterlinck shoulders
Percy Mackaye. Shakespeare is between
Sardou and Shaw. Euripides and Clyde
Fitch! Upton Sinclair and Sophocles!
Aeschylus and F. Anstey! D'Annunzio
and Richard Harding Davis! Augustus
Thomas and Tolstoi!

More alphabetical humor. Gerhart

Hauptman and Robert Hichens; Voltaire and Henry Van Dyke; Flaubert and John Fox, Jr.; Balzac and John Kendrick Bangs; Ostrovsky and E. Phillips Oppenheim; Elinor Glyn and Théophile Gautier; Joseph Conrad and Robert W. Chambers; Zola and Zangwill! . . .

Midway of my scant shelf of novels, between George Moore and Frank Norris, there is just room enough for the three volumes of "Derringforth," by Frank A. Munsey.

XXVII

Virtuous Vandalism

A hearing of Schumann's B flat symphony of late, otherwise a very caressing experience, was corrupted by the thought that music would be much the gainer if musicians could get over their superstitious reverence for the mere text of the musical classics. That reverence, indeed, is already subject to certain limitations; hands have been laid, at one time or another, upon most of the immortal oratorios, and even the awful name of Bach has not dissuaded certain German editors. But it still swathes the standard symphonies like some vast armor of rubber and angel food, and so imagination has to come to the aid of the flutes and fiddles when the band plays Schumann, Mozart, and even parts of Beethoven. One discerns, often quite clearly, what the reverend Master was aiming at, but just as often one fails to hear it in precise tones.

This is particularly true of Schumann,

whose deficiency in instrumental cunning has passed into proverb. And in the B flat symphony, his first venture into the epic form, his failures are most numerous. More than once, obviously attempting to roll up tone into a moving climax, he succeeds only in muddling his colors. I remember one place—at the moment I can't recall where it is—where the strings and the brass storm at one another in furious figures. The blast of the brass, as the vaudevillains say, gets across—but the fiddles merely scream absurdly. The whole passage suggests the bleating of sheep in the midst of a vast bellowing of bulls. Schumann overestimated the horsepower of fiddle music so far up the E string—or underestimated the full thrust of the trumpets. . . . Other such soft spots are well known.

Why, then, go on parroting *gaucheries* that Schumann himself, were he alive today, would have long since corrected? Why not call an ecumenical council, appoint a commission to see to such things, and then forget the sacrilege? As a self-elected delegate from *partibus infidelium,* I nominate Dr. Richard Strauss as chairman. When all is said and done, Strauss probably knows more about writing for orchestra than any other two men that ever lived, not excluding Wagner. Surely no living rival has anything to teach him. If, after hearing a new composition by Strauss, one turns to the music, one is invariably surprised to find how simple it is. The performance reveals so many purple moments, so staggering an array of lusciousness, that the ear is bemused into detecting scales and chords that never were on land or sea. What the exploratory eye subsequently discovers, perhaps, is no more than our stout and comfortable old friend, the highly well-born *Hausfrau,* Mme. C Dur—with a vine leaf or two of C sharp minor or F major in her hair. The trick lies in the tone-color—in the flabbergasting magic of the orchestration. There are some moments in "Elektra" when sounds come out of the orchestra that tug at the very roots of the hair, sounds so unearthly that they suggest a caroling of dragons or *Bierfisch*—and yet they are made by the same old fiddles that play the Kaiser Quartette, and by the same old trombones that the Valkyrie ride like witch's broomsticks, and by the same old flutes that sob and snuffle in Tit'l's Serenade. And in parts of "Feuersnot"—but Roget must be rewritten by Strauss before "Feuersnot" is described. There is one place where the harps, taking a running start from the scrolls of the violins, leap slambang through (or is it into?) the firmament of Heaven. Once, when I heard this passage played at a concert, a fat woman sitting beside me rolled over like a perfumed ox, and had to be hauled out by the ushers.

Yes; Strauss is the man to reorchestrate the symphonies of Schumann, particularly the B flat and the Fourth. I doubt that he could do much with Schubert, for Schubert, though he is dead nearly a hundred years, yet remains curiously modern. The Unfinished symphony is full of exquisite color effects—consider, for example, the rustling figure for the strings in the first movement—and as for the C major, it is so stupendous a debauch of melodic and harmonic beauty that one scarcely notices the colors at all. In its slow movement mere loveliness in music probably says all that will ever be said. . . . But what of old Ludwig? Har, har; here we begin pulling the whiskers of Baal Himself. Nevertheless, I am vandal enough to wonder, on sad Sunday mornings, what Strauss could do with the first movement of the C minor. More, if Strauss ever does it and lets me hear the result just once, I'll be glad to serve six months in jail with him. . . . But in Munich, of course! And with a daily visitor's pass for Cousin Pschorr! . . .

XXVIII

A Footnote on the Duel of Sex

If I were a woman I should want to be
a blonde, with golden, silky hair, pink
cheeks and sky-blue eyes. It would not
bother me to think that this color scheme
was mistaken by the world for a flaunting
badge of stupidity; I would have a better
arm in my arsenal than mere intelligence;
I would get a husband by easy surrender
while the brunettes attempted it vainly by
frontal assault.

Men are not easily taken by frontal
assault; it is only strategem that can
quickly knock them down. To be a
blonde, pink, soft and delicate, is to be a
strategem. It is to be a ruse, a feint, an
ambush. It is to fight under the Red
Cross flag. A man sees nothing alert and
designing in those pale, crystalline eyes;
he sees only something helpless, childish,
weak; something that calls to his compassion; something that appeals powerfully
to his conceit in his own strength. And

82

so he is taken before he knows that there is a war. He lifts his portcullis in Christian charity—and the enemy is in his citadel.

The brunette can make no such stealthy and sure attack. No matter how subtle her art, she can never hope to quite conceal her intent. Her eyes give her away. They flash and glitter. They have depths. They draw the male gaze into mysterious and sinister recesses. And so the male behind the gaze flies to arms. He may be taken in the end—indeed, he usually is—but he is not taken by surprise; he is not taken without a fight. A brunette has to battle for every inch of her advance. She is confonted by an endless succession of Dead Man's Hills, each equipped with telescopes, semaphores, alarm gongs, wireless. The male sees her clearly through her densest smoke clouds. . . . But the blonde captures him under a flag of truce. He regards her tenderly, kindly, almost pityingly, until the moment the gyves are upon his wrists.

It is all an optical matter, a question of color. The pastel shades deceive him; the louder hues send him to his artillery. God help, I say, the red-haired girl! She goes into action with warning pennants flying. The dullest, blindest man can see her a mile away; he can catch the alarming flash of her hair long before he can see the whites, or even the terrible red-browns, of her eyes. She has a long field to cross, heavily under defensive fire, before she can get into rifle range. Her quarry has a chance to throw up redoubts, to dig himself in, to call for reinforcements, to elude her by ignominious flight. She must win, if she is to win at all, by an unparalleled combination of craft and resolution. She must be swift, daring, merciless. Even the brunette of black and penetrating eye has great advantages over her. No wonder she never lets go, once her arms are around her antagonist's neck! No wonder she is, of all women, the hardest to shake off!

All nature works in circles. Causes become effects; effects develop into causes. The red-haired girl's dire need of courage and cunning has augmented her store of those qualities by the law of natural selection. She is, by long odds, the most intelligent and bemusing of women. She shows cunning, foresight, technique, variety. She always fails a dozen times before she succeeds; but she brings to the final business the abominable expertness of a Ludendorff; she has learnt painfully by the process of trial and error. Red-haired girls are intellectual stimulants. They know all the tricks. They are so clever that they have even cast a false glamour of beauty about their worst defect—their harsh and gaudy hair. They give it euphemistic and deceitful names— auburn, bronze, Titian. They overcome by their hellish arts that deep-seated dread of red which is inborn in all of God's creatures. They charm men with what would even alarm bulls.

And the blondes, by following the law of least resistance, have gone in the other

direction. The great majority of them—
I speak, of course, of natural blondes; not
of the immoral wenches who work their
atrocities under cover of a synthetic
blondeness—are quite as shallow and
stupid as they look. One seldom hears a
blonde say anything worth hearing; the
most they commonly achieve is a specious,
baby-like prattling, an infantile artless-
ness. But let us not blame them for nature's work. Why, after all, be intelligent? It is, at best, no more than a capacity for unhappiness. The blonde not only
doesn't miss it; she is even better off without it. What imaginable intelligence
could compensate her for the flat blue-
ness of her eyes, the xanthous pallor of
her hair, the doll-like pink of her cheeks?
What conceivable cunning could do such
execution as her stupendous appeal to
masculine vanity, sentimentality, egoism?

If I were a woman I should want to be
a blonde. My blondeness might be hideous, but it would get me a husband, and
it would make him cherish me and love
me.

86

XXIX

ALCOHOL

Envy, as I have said, is at the heart of the messianic delusion, the mania to convert the happy sinner into a "good" man, and so make him miserable. And at the heart of that envy is fear—the fear to sin, to take a chance, to monkey with the buzz-saw. This ineradicable fear is the outstanding mark of the fifth-rate man, at all times and everywhere. It dominates his politics, his theology, his whole thinking. He is a moral fellow because he is afraid to venture over the fence—and he hates the man who is not.

The solemn proofs, so laboriously deduced from life insurance statistics, that the man who uses alcohol, even moderately, dies slightly sooner than the teetotaler—these proofs merely show that this man is one who leads an active and vigorous life, and so faces hazards and uses himself up—in brief, one who lives at high tempo and with full joy, what

Nietzsche used to call the *Ja-Sager,* or
yes-sayer. He may, in fact, die slightly
sooner than the teetotaler, but he lives infinitely longer. Moreover, his life,
humanly speaking, is much more worth
while, to himself and to the race. He
does the hard and dangerous work of the
world, he takes the chances, he makes the
experiments. He is the soldier, the artist,
the innovator, the lover. All the great
works of man have been done by men
who thus lived joyously, strenuously, and
perhaps a bit dangerously. They have
never been concerned about stretching life
for two or three more years; they have
been concerned about making life engrossing and stimulating and a high adventure
while it lasts. Teetotalism is as impossible
to such men as any other manifestation
of cowardice, and, if it were possible, it
would destroy their utility and significance just as certainly.

A man who shrinks from a cocktail before dinner on the ground it may flab-
bergast his hormones, and so make him

die at 69 years, ten months and five days
instead of at 69 years, eleven months and
seven days, such a man is as absurd a poltroon as the fellow who shrinks from kissing a woman on the ground that she may
floor him with a chair leg. Each flees from
a purely theoretical risk. Each is a use-
less encumberer of the earth, and the
sooner dead the better. Each is a dis-
credit to the human race, already discred-
itable enough, God knows.

Teetotalism does not make for human
happiness; it makes for the dull, idiotic
happiness of the barnyard. The men who
do things in the world, the men worthy
of admiration and imitation are men con-
stitutionally incapable of any such peck-
sniffian stupidity. Their ideal is not a
safe life, but a full life; they do not try
to follow the canary bird in a cage, but
the eagle in the air. And in particular
they do not flee from shadows and bug-
aboos. The alcohol myth is such a
bugaboo. The sort of man it scares is the

sort of man whose chief mark is that he is always scared.

No wonder the Rockefellers and their like are hot for saving the workingman from John Barleycorn! Imagine the advantage to them of operating upon a flabby horde of timorous and joyless slaves, afraid of all fun and kicking up, horribly moral, eager only to live as long as possible! What mule-like fidelity and efficiency could be got out of such a rabble! But how many Lincolns would you get out of it, and how many Jacksons, and how many Grants?

XXX

Thoughts on the Voluptuous

Why has no publisher ever thought of
perfuming his novels? The final refine-
ment of publishing, already bedizened by
every other art! Barabbas turned Petro-
nius! For instance, consider the bucolic
romances of the hyphenated Mrs. Porter.
They have a subtle flavor of new-mown
hay and daffodils already; why not add
the actual essence, or at all events some
safe coal-tar substitute, and so help
imagination to spread its wings? For
Hall Caine, musk and synthetic bergamot.
For Mrs. Glyn and her neighbors on the
tiger-skin, the fragrant blood of the red,
red rose. For the ruffianish pages of Jack
London, the pungent, hospitable smell of
a first-class bar-room—that indescribable
mingling of Maryland rye, cigar smoke,
stale malt liquor, radishes, potato salad
and *Blutwurst*. For the Dartmoor sagas
of the interminable Phillpotts, the warm
ammoniacal bouquet of cows, poultry and

yokels. For the "Dodo" school, violets
and Russian cigarettes. For the venerable
Howells, lavender and mignonette. For
Zola, Rochefort and wet leather. For
Mrs. Humphrey Ward, lilies of the val-
ley. For Marie Corelli, tuberoses and
embalming fluid. For Chambers, sachet
and lip paint. For——

But I leave you to make your own
choices. All I offer is the general idea.
It has been tried in the theatre. Well do
I remember the first weeks of "Floro-
dora" at the old Casino, with a mannikin
in the lobby squirting "La Flor de Floro-
dora" upon all us Florodorans. . . . I was
put on trial for my life when I got home!

XXXI

The Holy Estate

Marriage is always a man's second choice. It is entered upon, more often *y* than not, as the safest form of intrigue. The caitiff yields quickest; the man who loves danger and adventure holds out longest. Behind it one frequently finds, not that lofty romantic passion which poets hymn, but a mere yearning for peace and security. The abominable hazards of the high seas, the rough humors and pestilences of the forecastle—these drive the timid mariner ashore. . . . The authentic Cupid, at least in Christendom, was discovered by the late Albert Ludwig Siegmund Neisser in 1879.

XXXII

DICHTUNG UND WAHRHEIT

Deponent, being duly sworn, saith: My taste in poetry is for delicate and fragile things—to be honest, for artificial things. I like a frail but perfectly articulated stanza, a sonnet wrought like ivory, a song full of glowing nouns, verbs, adjectives, adverbs, pronouns, conjunctions, prepositions and participles, but without too much hard sense to it. Poetry, to me, has but two meanings. On the one hand, it is a magical escape from the sordidness of metabolism and the class war, and on the other hand it is a subtle, very difficult and hence very charming art, like writing fugues or mixing mayonnaise. I do not go to poets to be taught anything, or to be heated up to indignation, or to have my conscience blasted out of its torpor, but to be soothed and caressed, to be lulled with sweet sounds, to be wooed into forgetfulness, to be tickled under the metaphysical chin. My favorite poem is Lizette Woodworth Roose's "Tears," which, as a statement of fact, seems to me to be as idiotic as the Book of Revelation. The poetry I regard least is such stuff as that of Robert Browning and Matthew Arnold, which argues and illuminates. I dislike poetry of intellectual content as much as I dislike women of intellectual content—and for the same reason.

XXXIII

WILD SHOTS

If I had the time, and there were no sweeter follies offering, I should like to write an essay on the books that have quite failed of achieving their original purposes, and are yet of respectable use and potency for other purposes. For example, the Book of Revelation. The obvious aim of the learned author of this work was to bring the early Christians into accord by telling them authoritatively what to expect and hope for; its actual effect during eighteen hundred years has been to split them into a multitude of camps, and so set them to denouncing, damning, jailing, and murdering one another. Again, consider the autobiography of Benvenuto Cellini. Ben wrote it to prove that he was an honest man, a mirror of all the virtues, an injured innocent; the world, reading it, hails him respectfully as the noblest, the boldest, the gaudiest liar that ever lived. Again, turn to "Gul-

96

liver's Travels." The thing was planned by its rev. author as a devastating satire, a terrible piece of cynicism; it survives as a storybook for sucklings. Yet again, there is "Hamlet." Shakespeare wrote it frankly to make money for a theatrical manager; it has lost money for theatrical managers ever since. Yet again, there is Cæsar's "De Bello Gallico." Julius composed it to thrill and arouse the Romans; its sole use today is to stupefy and sicken schoolboys. Finally, there is the celebrated book of General F. von Bernhardi. He wrote it to inflame Germany; its effect was to inflame England. . . .

The list might be lengthened almost *ad infinitum*. When a man writes a book he fires a machine gun into a wood. The game he brings down often astonishes him, and sometimes horrifies him. Consider the case of Ibsen. . . . After my book on Nietzsche I was actually invited to lecture at Princeton.

XXXIV

BEETHOVEN

Romain Rolland's "Beethoven," one of
the cornerstones of his celebrity as a
critic, is based upon a thesis that is of almost inconceivable inaccuracy, to wit, the
thesis that old Ludwig was an apostle
of joy, and that his music reveals his determination to experience and utter it in
spite of all the slings and arrows of out-
rageous fortune. Nothing could be more
absurd. Joy, in truth, was precisely the
emotion that Beethoven could never conjure up; it simply was not in him. Turn
to the *scherzo* of any of his trios, quartets,
sonatas or symphonies. A sardonic wag-
gishness is there, and sometimes even a
wistful sort of merriment, but joy in the
real sense—a kicking up of legs, a light-
heartedness, a complete freedom from
care—is not to be found. It is in Haydn,
it is in Schubert and it is often in Mozart,
but it is no more in Beethoven than it is in
Tchaikovsky. Even the hymn to joy at the

end of the Ninth symphony narrowly escapes being a gruesome parody on the thing itself; a conscious effort is in every note of it; it is almost as lacking in spontaneity as (if it were imaginable at all) a piece of *vers libre* by Augustus Montague Toplady.

Nay; Ludwig was no leaping buck. Nor was it his deafness, nor poverty, nor the crimes of his rascally nephew that pumped joy out of him. The truth is that he lacked it from birth; he was born a Puritan—and though a Puritan may also become a great man (as witness Herbert Spencer and Beelzebub), he can never throw off being a Puritan. Beethoven stemmed from the Low Countries, and the Low Countries, in those days, were full of Puritan refugees; the very name, in its first incarnation, may have been Barebones. If you want to comprehend the authentic man, don't linger over Rolland's fancies but go to his own philosophizings, as garnered in "Beethoven, the Man and the Artist," by Friedrich Kerst. Here you will find a collection of moral banalities that would have delighted Jonathan Edwards—a collection that might well be emblazoned on gilt cards and hung in Sunday schools. He begins with a naif anthropomorphism that is now almost perished from the world; he ends with a solemn repudiation of adultery. . . . But a great man, my masters, a great man! We have enough biographies of him, and talmuds upon his works. Who will do a full-length psychological study of him?

XXXV

THE TONE ART

The notion that the aim of art is to fix the shifting aspects of nature, that all art is primarily representative—this notion is as unsound as the theory that Friday is an unlucky day, and is dying as hard. One even finds some trace of it in Anatole France, surely a man who should know better. The true function of art is to criticise, embellish and edit nature—particularly to edit it, and so make it coherent and lovely. The artist is a sort of impassioned proof-reader, blue-pencilling the bad spelling of God. The sounds in a Beethoven symphony, even the Pastoral, are infinitely more orderly, varied and beautiful than those of the woods. The worst flute is never as bad as the worst soprano. The best violincello is immeasurably better than the best tenor.

All first-rate music suffers by the fact that it has to be performed by human beings—that is, that nature must be per-

mitted to corrupt it. The performance
one hears in a concert hall or opera house
is no more than a baroque parody upon
the thing the composer imagined. In an
orchestra of eighty men there is inevitably at least one man with a sore thumb,
or bad kidneys, or an anthropophagous
wife, or *Katzerjammer* — and one is
enough. Some day the natural clumsiness
and imperfection of fingers, lips and
larynxes will be overcome by mechanical
devices, and we shall have Beethoven and
Mozart and Schubert in such wonderful
and perfect beauty that it will be almost
unbearable. If half as much ingenuity
had been lavished upon music machines
as has been lavished upon the telephone
and the steam engine, we would have had
mechanical orchestras long ago. Mechanical pianos are already here. Piano-play-
ers, bound to put some value on the tortures of Czerny, affect to laugh at all such
contrivances, but that is no more than a
pale phosphorescence of an outraged
Wille zur Macht. Setting aside half a

dozen—perhaps a dozen—great masters of a moribund craft, who will say that the average mechanical piano is not as competent as the average pianist?

When the human performer of music goes the way of the galley-slave, the charm of personality, of course, will be pumped out of the performance of music. But the charm of personality does not help music; it hinders it. It is not a reinforcement to music; it is a rival. When a beautiful singer comes upon the stage, two shows, as it were, go on at once: first the music show, and then the arms, shoulders, neck, nose, ankles, eyes, hips, calves and ruby lips—in brief, the sex-show. The second of these shows, to the majority of persons present, is more interesting than the first—to the men because of the sex interest, and to the women because of the professional or technical interest—and so music is forced into the background. What it becomes, indeed, is no more than a half-heard accompaniment to an imagined anecdote, just as color, line and

103

mass become mere accomplishments to an anecdote in a picture by an English academician, or by a sentimental German of the Boecklin school.

The purified and dephlogisticated music of the future, to be sure, will never appeal to the mob, which will keep on demanding its chance to gloat over gaudy, voluptuous women, and fat, scandalous tenors. The mob, even disregarding its insatiable appetite for the improper, is a natural hero worshipper. It loves, not the beautiful, but the strange, the unprecedented, the astounding; it suffers from an incurable *héliogabalisme*. A soprano who can gargle her way up to G sharp in altissimo interests it almost as much as a contralto who has slept publicly with a grand duke. If it cannot get the tenor who receives $3,000 a night, it will take the tenor who fought the manager with bung-starters last Tuesday. But this is merely saying that the tastes and desires of the mob have nothing to do with music as an art. For its ears, for its eyes, it demands anecdotes—on the one hand the Suicide symphony, "The Forge in the Forest," and the general run of Italian opera, and on the other hand such things as "The Angelus," "Playing Grandpa" and the so-called "Mona Lisa." It cannot imagine art as devoid of moral content, as beauty pure and simple. It always demands something to edify it, or, failing that, to shock it.

These concepts, of the edifying and the shocking, are closer together in the psyche than most persons imagine. The one, in fact, depends upon the other: without some definite notion of the improving it is almost impossible to conjure up an active notion of the improper. All salacious art is addressed, not to the damned, but to the consciously saved; it is Sunday-school superintendents, not bartenders, who chiefly patronize peep-shows, and know the dirty books, and have a high regard for sopranos of superior gluteal development. The man who has risen above the petty ethical superstitions of

105

Christendom gets little pleasure out of impropriety, for very few ordinary phenomena seem to him to be improper. Thus a Frenchman, viewing the undraped statues which bedizen his native galleries of art, either enjoys them in a purely æsthetic fashion— which is seldom possible save when he is in liquor—or confesses frankly that he doesn't like them at all; whereas the visiting Americano is so powerfully shocked and fascinated by them that one finds him, the same evening, in places where no respectable man ought to go. All art, to this fellow, must have a certain bawdiness, or he cannot abide it. His favorite soprano, in the opera house, is not the fat and middle-aged lady who can actually sing, but the girl with the bare back and translucent drawers. Condescending to the concert hall, he is bored by the posse of enemy aliens in funereal black, and so demands a vocal soloist— that is, a gaudy creature of such advanced corsetting that she can make him forget

Bach for a while, and turn his thoughts pleasantly to amorous intrigue.

In all this, of course, there is nothing new. Other and better men have noted the damage that the personal equation does to music, and some of them have even sought ways out. For example, Richard Strauss. His so-called ballet, "Josefs Legend," produced in Paris just before the war, is an attempt to write an opera without singers. All of the music is in the orchestra; the folks on the stage merely go through a pointless pantomime; their main function is to entertain the eye with shifting colors. Thus, the romantic sentiments of Joseph are announced, not by some eye-rolling tenor, but by the first, second, third, fourth, fifth, sixth, seventh and eighth violins (it is a Strauss score!), with the incidental aid of the wood-wind, the brass, the percussion and the rest of the strings. And the heroine's reply is made, not by a soprano with a cold, but by an honest man playing a flute. The next step will be the substitution of marionettes for actors. The removal of the orchestra to a sort of trench, out of sight of the audience, is already an accomplished fact at Munich. The end, perhaps, will be music purged of its current ptomaines. In brief, music.

XXXVI

Zoos

I often wonder how much sound and nourishing food is fed to the animals in the zoological gardens of America every week, and try to figure out what the public gets in return for the cost thereof. The annual bill must surely run into millions; one is constantly hearing how much beef a lion downs at a meal and how many tons of hay an elephant dispatches in a month. And to what end? To the end, principally, that a horde of superintendents and keepers may be kept in easy jobs. To the end, secondarily, that the least intelligent minority of the population may have an idiotic show to gape at on Sunday afternoons, and that the young of the species may be instructed in the methods of amour prevailing among chimpanzees and become privy to the technic employed by jaguars, hyenas and polar bears in ridding themselves of lice.

So far as I can make out, after labori-

ous visits to all the chief zoos of the nation,
no other imaginable purpose is served by
their existence. One hears constantly, true
enough (mainly from the gentlemen they
support) that they are educational. But
how? Just what sort of instruction do
they radiate, and what is its value? I
have never been able to find out. The
sober truth is that they are no more educational than so many firemen's parades
or displays of sky-rockets, and that all
they actually offer to the public in return
for the taxes wasted upon them is a form
of idle and witless amusement, compared
to which a visit to a penitentiary, or even
to Congress or a state legislature in session,
is informing, stimulating and ennobling.

Education your grandmother! Show
me a schoolboy who has ever learned anything valuable or important by watching
a mangy old lion snoring away in its cage
or a family of monkeys fighting for pea-
nuts. To get any useful instruction out of
such a spectacle is palpably impossible;
not even a college professor is improved

by it. The most it can imaginably impart is that the stripes of a certain sort of tiger run one way and the stripes of another sort some other way, that hyenas and polecats smell worse than Greek 'bus boys, that the Latin name of the raccoon (who was unheard of by the Romans) is *Procyon lotor.* For the dissemination of such banal knowledge, absurdly emitted and defectively taken in, the taxpayers of the United States are mulcted in hundreds of thousands of dollars a year. As well make them pay for teaching policemen the theory of least squares, or for instructing roosters in the laying of eggs.

But the zoos, it is argued, are of scientific value. They enable learned men to study this or that. Again the facts blast the theory. No scientific discovery of any value whatsoever, even to the animals themselves, has ever come out of a zoo. The zoo scientist is the old woman of zoology, and his alleged wisdom is usually exhibited, not in the groves of actual learning, but in the yellow journals. He

111

is to biology what the late Camille Flammarion was to astronomy, which is to say, its court jester and reductio ad absurdum. When he leaps into public notice with some new pearl of knowledge, it commonly turns out to be no more than the news that Marie Bashkirtseff, the Russian lady walrus, has had her teeth plugged with zinc and is expecting twins. Or that Pishposh, the man-eating alligator, is down with locomotor ataxia. Or that Damon, the grizzly, has just finished his brother Pythias in the tenth round, chewing off his tail, nose and remaining ear.

Science, of course, has its uses for the lower animals. A diligent study of their livers and lights helps to an understanding of the anatomy and physiology, and particularly of the pathology, of man. They are necessary aids in devising and manufacturing many remedial agents, and in testing the virtues of those already devised; out of the mute agonies of a rabbit or a calf may come relief for a baby with diphtheria, or means for an archdeacon to escape the consequences of his youthful follies. Moreover, something valuable is to be got out of a mere study of their habits, instincts and ways of mind —knowledge that, by analogy, may illuminate the parallel doings of the *genus homo,* and so enable us to comprehend the primitive mental processes of Congressmen, morons and the rev. clergy.

But it must be obvious that none of these studies can be made in a zoo. The zoo animals, to begin with, provide no material for the biologist; he can find out no more about their insides than what he discerns from a safe distance and through the bars. He is not allowed to try his germs and specifics upon them; he is not allowed to vivisect them. If he would find out what goes on in the animal body under this condition or that, he must turn from the inhabitants of the zoo to the customary guinea pigs and street dogs, and buy or steal them for himself. Nor does he get any chance for profitable inquiry when zoo animals die (usually of lack of exercise or ignorant doctoring), for their carcasses are not handed to him for autopsy, but at once stuffed with gypsum and excelsior and placed in some museum.

Least of all do zoos produce any new knowledge about animal behavior. Such knowledge must be got, not from animals penned up and tortured, but from animals in a state of nature. A college professor studying the habits of the giraffe, for example, and confining his observation to specimens in zoos, would inevitably come to the conclusions that the giraffe is a sedentary and melancholy beast, standing immovable for hours at a time and employing an Italian to feed him hay and cabbages. As well proceed to a study of the psychology of a jurisconsult by first immersing him in Sing Sing, or of a juggler by first cutting off his hands. Knowledge so gained is inaccurate and imbecile knowledge. Not even a college professor, if sober, would give it any faith and credit.

There remains, then, the only true util-

114

ity of a zoo: it is a childish and pointless show for the unintelligent, in brief, for children, nurse-maids, visiting yokels and the generality of the defective. Should the taxpayers be forced to sweat millions for such a purpose? I think not. The sort of man who likes to spend his time watching a cage of monkeys chase one another, or a lion gnaw its tail, or a lizard catch flies, is precisely the sort of man whose mental weakness should be combatted at the public expense, and not fostered. He is a public liability and a public menace, and society should seek to improve him. Instead of that, we spend a lot of money to feed his degrading appetite and further paralyze his mind. It is precisely as if the community provided free champagne for dipsomaniacs, or hired lecturers to convert the army to the doctrines of the Bolsheviki.

Of the abominable cruelties practised in zoos it is unnecessary to make mention. Even assuming that all the keepers are men of delicate nature and ardent zoö-

115

philes (which is about as safe as assuming that the keepers of a prison are all sentimentalists, and weep for the sorrows of their charges), it must be plain that the work they do involves an endless war upon the native instincts of the animals, and that they must thus inflict the most abominable tortures every day. What could be a sadder sight than a tiger in a cage, save it be a forest monkey climbing despairingly up a barked stump, or an eagle chained to its roost? How can man be benefitted and made better by robbing the seal of its arctic ice, the hippopotamus of its soft wallow, the buffalo of its open range, the lion of its kingship, the birds of their air?

I am no sentimentalist, God knows. I am in favor of vivisection unrestrained, so long as the vivisectionist knows what he is about. I advocate clubbing a dog that barks unnecesarily, which all dogs do. I enjoy hangings, particularly of converts to the evangelical faiths. I once poisoned a clergyman. The crunch of a cockroach is music to my ears. But when the day comes to turn the prisoners of the zoo out of their cages, if it is only to lead them to the swifter, kinder knife of the *schochet,* I shall be present and rejoicing, and if any one present thinks to suggest that it would be a good plan to celebrate the day by shooting the whole zoo faculty, I shall have a revolver in my pocket and a sound eye in my head.

XXXVII

On Hearing Mozart

The only permanent values in the world are truth and beauty, and of these it is probable that truth is lasting only in so far as it is a function and manifestation of beauty—a projection of feeling in terms of idea. The world is a charnel house of dead religions. Where are all the faiths of the middle ages, so complex and yet so precise? But all that was essential in the beauty of the middle ages still lives. . . .

This is the heritage of man, but not of men. The great majority of men are not even aware of it. Their participation in the progress of the world, and even in the history of the world, is infinitely remote and trivial. They live and die, at bottom, as animals live and die. The human race, as a race, is scarcely cognizant of their existence; they haven't even definite number, but stand grouped together as x, the quantity unknown . . . and not worth knowing.

XXXVIII

The Road to Doubt

The first effect of what used to be called natural philosophy is to fill its devotee with wonder at the marvels of God. This explains why the pursuit of science, so long as it remains superficial, is not incompatible with the most naïve sort of religious faith. But the moment the student of the sciences passes this stage of childlike amazement and begins to investigate the inner workings of natural phenomena, he begins to see how ineptly many of them are managed, and so he tends to pass from awe of the Creator to criticism of the Creator, and once he has crossed that bridge he has ceased to be a believer. One finds plenty of neighborhood physicians, amateur botanists, high-school physics teachers and other such quasi-scientists in the pews on Sunday, but one never sees a Huxley there, or a Darwin, or an Ehrlich.

XXXIX

A New Use for Churches

The argument by design, it may be granted, establishes a reasonable ground for accepting the existence of God. It makes belief, at all events, quite as intelligible as unbelief. But when the theologians take their step from the existence of God to the goodness of God they tread upon much less firm earth. How can one see any proof of that goodness in the senseless and intolerable sufferings of man—his helplessness, the brief and troubled span of his life, the inexplicable disproportion between his deserts and his rewards, the tragedy of his soaring aspiration, the worse tragedy of his dumb questioning? Granting the existence of God, a house dedicated to Him naturally follows. He is all-important; it is fit that man should take some notice of Him. But why praise and flatter him for his unspeakable cruelties? Why forget so supinely His failures to remedy the easily remediable? Why, indeed, devote the churches exclusively to worship? Why not give them over, now and then, to justifiable indignation meetings?

Perhaps men will incline to this idea later on. It is not inconceivable, indeed, that religion will one day cease to be a poltroonish acquiescence and become a vigorous and insistent criticism. If God can hear a petition, what ground is there for holding that He would not hear a complaint? It might, indeed, please Him to find His creatures grown so self-reliant and reflective. More, it might even help Him to get through His infinitely complex and difficult work. Theology has already moved toward such notions. It has abandoned the primitive doctrine of God's arbitrariness and indifference, and substituted the doctrine that He is willing, and even eager, to hear the desires of His creatures—*i. e.,* their private notions, born of experience, as to what would be best for them. Why assume that those notions would be any the less worth hearing and

121

heeding if they were cast in the form of criticism, and even of denunciation? Why hold that the God who can understand and forgive even treason could not understand and forgive remonstrance?

XL

The Root of Religion

The idea of literal truth crept into religion relatively late: it is the invention of lawyers, priests and cheese-mongers. The idea of mystery long preceded it, and at the heart of that idea of mystery was an idea of beauty—that is, an idea that this or that view of the celestial and infernal process presented a satisfying picture of form, rhythm and organization. Once this view was adopted as satisfying, its professional interpreters and their dupes sought to reinforce it by declaring it true. The same flow of reasoning is familiar on lower planes. The average man does not get pleasure out of an idea because he thinks it is true; he thinks it is true because he gets pleasure out of it.

XLI

Free Will

Free will, it appears, is still a Christian
dogma. Without it the cruelties of God
would strain faith to the breaking-point.
But outside the fold it is gradually falling
into decay. Such men of science as George
W. Crile and Jacques Loeb have dealt it
staggering blows, and among laymen of
inquiring mind it seems to be giving way
to an apologetic sort of determinism—a
determinism, one may say, tempered by
defective observation. The late Mark
Twain, in his secret heart, was such a determinist. In his "What Is Man?" you
will find him at his farewells to libertarianism. The vast majority of our acts, he
argues, are determined, but there remains
a residuum of free choices. Here we stand
free of compulsion and face a pair or more
of alternatives, and are free to go this way
or that.

A pillow for free will to fall upon—
but one loaded with disconcerting brick-

bats. Where the occupants of this last trench of libertarianism err is in their assumption that the pulls of their antagonistic impulses are exactly equal—that the individual is absolutely free to choose which one he will yield to. Such freedom, in practise, is never encountered. When an individual confronts alternatives, it is not alone his volition that chooses between them, but also his environment, his inherited prejudices, his race, his color, his condition of servitude. I may kiss a girl or I may not kiss her, but surely it would be absurd to say that I am, in any true sense, a free agent in the matter. The world has even put my helplessness into a proverb. It says that my decision and act depend upon the time, the place—and even to some extent, upon the girl.

Examples might be multiplied *ad infinitum*. I can scarcely remember performing a wholly voluntary act. My whole life, as I look back upon it, seems to be a long series of inexplicable accidents, not only quite unavoidable, but even quite un-

intelligible. Its history is the history of
the reactions of my personality to my environment, of my behavior before exter-
nal stimuli. I have been no more respon-
sible for that personality than I have been
for that environment. To say that I can
change the former by a voluntary effort
is as ridiculous as to say that I can modify
the curvature of the lenses of my eyes. I
know, because I have often tried to change
it, and always failed. Nevertheless, it has
changed. I am not the same man I was
in the last century. But the gratifying im-
provements so plainly visible are surely
not to be credited to me. All of them
came from without—or from unplumb-
able and uncontrollable depths within.

The more the matter is examined the
more the residuum of free will shrinks and
shrinks, until in the end it is almost impossible to find it. A great many men, of
course, looking at themselves, see it as
something very large; they slap their
chests and call themselves free agents, and
demand that God reward them for their

virtue. But these fellows are simply idiotic egoists, devoid of a critical sense. They mistake the acts of God for their own acts. Of such sort are the coxcombs who boast about wooing and winning their wives. They are brothers to the fox who boasted that he had made the hounds run. . . .

The throwing overboard of free will is commonly denounced on the ground that it subverts morality and makes of religion a mocking. Such pious objections, of course, are foreign to logic, but nevertheless, it may be well to give a glance to this one. It is based upon the fallacious hypothesis that the determinist escapes, or hope to escape, the consequences of his acts. Nothing could be more untrue. Consequences follow acts just as relentlessly if the latter be involuntary as if they be voluntary. If I rob a bank of my free choice or in response to some unfathomable inner necessity it is all one; I will go to the same jail. Conscripts in war are killed just as often as volunteers. Men

127

who are tracked down and shanghaied by their wives have just as hard a time of it as men who walk fatuously into the trap by formally proposing.

Even on the ghostly side, determinism does not do much damage to theology. It is no harder to believe that a man will be damned for his involuntary acts than it is to believe that he will be damned for his voluntary acts, for even the supposition that he is wholly free does not dispose of the massive fact that God made him as he is, and that God could have made him a saint if He had so desired. To deny this is to flout omnipotence—a crime at which, as I have often said, I balk. But here I begin to fear that I wade too far into the hot waters of the sacred sciences, and that I had better retire before I lose my hide. This prudent retirement is purely deterministic. I do not ascribe it to my own sagacity; I ascribe it wholly to that singular kindness which fate always shows me. If I were free I'd probably keep on, and then regret it afterward.

XLII

Quid Est Veritas?

All great religions, in order to escape
absurdity, have to admit a dilution of agnosticism. It is only the savage, whether
of the African bush or the American gospel tent, who pretends to know the will
and intent of God exactly and completely.
"For who hath known the mind of the
Lord?" asked Paul of the Romans. "How
unsearchable are his judgments, and his
ways past finding out!" "It is the glory
of God," said Solomon, "to conceal a
thing." "Clouds and darkness," said
David, "are around him." "No man,"
said the Preacher, "can find out the work
of God." . . . The difference between religions is a difference in their relative content of agnosticism. The most satisfying
and ecstatic faith is almost purely agnos-
tic. It trusts absolutely without profess-
ing to know at all.

129

XLIII

THE DOUBTER'S REWARD

Despite the common delusion to the
contrary the philosophy of doubt is far
more comforting than that of hope. The
doubter escapes the worst penalty of the
man of hope; he is never disappointed,
and hence never indignant. The inexplicable and irremediable may interest
him, but they do not enrage him, or, I
may add, fool him. This immunity is
worth all the dubious assurances ever
foisted upon man. It is pragmatically im-
pregnable. . . . Moreover, it makes for
tolerance and sympathy. The doubter does
not hate his opponents; he sympathizes
with them. In the end, he may even come
to sympathize with God. . . . The old idea
of fatherhood here submerges in a new
idea of brotherhood. God, too, is beset by
limitations, difficulties, broken hopes. Is
it disconcerting to think of Him thus?
Well, is it any the less disconcerting to

think of Him as able to ease and answer, and yet failing? . . .

But he that doubteth—*damnatus est.* At once the penalty of doubt—and its proof, excuse and genesis.

XLIV

Before the Altar

A salient objection to the prevailing religious ceremonial lies in the attitudes of abasement that it enforces upon the faithful. A man would be thought a slimy and knavish fellow if he approached any human judge or potentate in the manner provided for approaching the Lord God. It is an etiquette that involves loss of self-respect, and hence it cannot be pleasing to its object, for one cannot think of the Lord God as sacrificing decent feelings to mere vanity. This notion of abasement, like most of the other ideas that are general in the world, is obviously the invention of small and ignoble men. It is the pollution of theology by the *Sklavenmoral*.

XLV

The Mask

Ritual is to religion what the music of an opera is to the libretto: ostensibly a means of interpretation, but actually a means of concealment. The Presbyterians made the mistake of keeping the doctrine of infant damnation in plain words. As enlightenment grew in the world, intelligence and prudery revolted against it, and so it had to be abandoned. Had it been set to music it would have survived— uncomprehended, unsuspected and unchallenged.

XLVI

PIA VENEZIANI, POI CRISTIANI

I have spoken of the possibility that
God, too, may suffer from a finite intelligence, and so know the bitter sting of dis-
appointment and defeat. Here I yielded
something to politeness; the thing is not
only possible, but obvious. Like man, God
is deceived by appearances and probabil-
ities; He makes calculations that do not
work out; He falls into specious assump-
tions. For example, He assumed that
Adam and Eve would obey the law in the
Garden. Again, He assumed that the ap-
palling lesson of the Flood would make
men better. Yet again, He assumed that
men would always put religion in first
place among their concerns—that it would
be eternally possible to reach and influence them through it. This last assumption was the most erroneous of them all.
The truth is that the generality of men have
long since ceased to take religion seriously.
When we encounter one who still does so,

he seems eccentric, almost feeble-minded
—or, more commonly, a rogue who has
been deluded by his own hypocrisy. Even
men who are professionaly religious, and
who thus have far more incentive to stick
to religion than the rest of us, nearly always throw it overboard at the first serious temptation. During the past four
years, for example, Christianity has been
in combat with patriotism all over Christendom. Which has prevailed? How
many gentlemen of God, having to choose
between Christ and Patrie, have actually
chosen Christ?

XLVII

OFF AGAIN, ON AGAIN

The ostensible object of the Reformation, which lately reached its fourth centenary, was to purge the Church of imbecilities. That object was accomplished; the Church shook them off. But imbecilities make an irresistible appeal to man; he inevitably tries to preserve them by cloaking them with religious sanctions. The result is Protestantism.

XLVIII

THEOLOGY

The notion that theology is a dull subject is one of the strangest delusions of a
stupid and uncritical age. The truth is
that some of the most engrossing books
ever written in the world are full of it.
For example, the Gospel according to
St. Luke. For example, Nietzsche's "Der
Antichrist." For example, Mark Twain's
"What Is Man?", St. Augustine's Confes-
sions, Haeckel's "The Riddle of the Uni-
verse," and Huxley's Essays. How, indeed, could a thing be dull that has sent
hundreds of thousands of men—the very
best and the very worst of the race—to the
gallows and the stake, and made and
broken dynasties, and inspired the greatest of human hopes and enterprises, and
embroiled whole continents in war? No,
theology is not a soporific. The reason it
so often seems so is that its public exposi-
tion has chiefly fallen, in these later days,
into the hands of a sect of intellectual cas-

137

trati, who begin by mistaking it for a sub-
department of etiquette, and then proceed
to anoint it with butter, rose water and
talcum powder. Whenever a first-rate intellect tackles it, as in the case of Huxley,
or in that of Leo XIII., it at once takes
on all the sinister fascination it had in
Luther's day.

XLIX

Exempli Gratia

Do I let the poor suffer, and consign them, as old Friedrich used to say, to statistics and the devil? Well, so does God.

LaVergne, TN USA
21 March 2011
221014LV00003B/49/P